SCIENCE ANSWERS

Solids, Liquids, and Gases

FROM ICE CUBES TO BUBBLES

Heinemann
LIBRARY

www.heinemann.co.uk/library

Visit our website to find out more information about **Heinemann Library** books.

To order:

☎ Phone 44 (0) 1865 888066

▤ Send a fax to 44 (0) 1865 314091

▣ Visit the Heinemann Bookshop at www.heinemann.co.uk/library to browse our catalogue and order online.

First published in Great Britain by Heinemann Library, Halley Court, Jordan Hill, Oxford OX2 8EJ, part of Harcourt Education.

Heinemann is a registered trademark of Harcourt Education Ltd.

Editorial: Sarah Eason and Georga Godwin
Design: Jo Hinton-Malivoire and
  Tinstar Design Ltd (www.tinstar.co.uk)
Illustrations: Jeff Edwards
Picture Research: Rosie Garai
  and Liz Eddison
Production: Viv Hichens

Originated by Ambassador Litho Ltd
Printed and bound in China by WKT

ISBN 0 431 17491 1 (hardback)
07 06 05 04 03
10 9 8 7 6 5 4 3 2 1

ISBN 0 431 17499 7 (paperback)
08 07 06 05 04
10 9 8 7 6 5 4 3 2 1

British Library Cataloguing in Publication Data

Ballard, Carol
Solids, liquids and gases. – (Science Answers)
530.4
A full catalogue record for this book is available from the British Library.

Acknowledgements

The Publishers would like to thank the following for permission to reproduce photographs: Corbis/Annie Griffiths Belt **p. 13**; Corbis/Donna Day **p. 23**; Corbis/ Tom Stewart **p. 21**; Liz Eddison **pp. 4, 5, 27**; Photodisc **p. 6**; Science Photo Library **p. 15, 28 (bottom), 28 (top)**; Science Photo Library/Sheila Terry **p. 28 (middle)**; Science Photo Library/Charles D. Winters **p. 16**; Science Photo Library/Phil Jude **p. 14**; Taxi/Getty Images/Packert White **p. 12**; Trevor Clifford **pp. 8, 11, 17, 22, 26**; Tudor Photography **p. 24**.

Cover photograph of the Pahoehoe lava flow, Kilauea Volcano, Hawaii reproduced with permission of Getty Images/ G. Brad Lewis.

The Publishers would like to thank Robert Snedden and Barbara Katz for their assistance with the preparation of this book.

Every effort has been made to contact copyright holders of any material reproduced in this book. Any omissions will be rectified in subsequent printings if notice is given to the Publishers.

Contents

Any words appearing in bold, **like this**, are explained in the Glossary.

About the experiments and demonstrations

In each chapter of this book you will find a section called 'Science Answers'. This describes an experiment or demonstration that you can try yourself. There are some simple safety rules to follow when doing an experiment:

• Ask an adult to help with any cutting using a sharp knife.
• Mains electricity is dangerous. Never, ever try to experiment with it.
• Do not use any of your experimental materials near a mains electrical socket.

Materials you will use

Most of the experiments and demonstrations in this book can be done with objects that you can find in your own home. A few will need items that you can buy from a hardware shop. You will also need paper and pencil to record your results.

What are solids, liquids and gases?

The **states of matter** are solid, liquid and gas. There are solids, liquids and gases all around us. Wood, metal, plastic and stone are all solids. Water, ink, blood and orange juice are all liquids. The air is a mixture of different gases. Solids, liquids and gases move and change in different ways and have different uses.

Using solids

We use solid **materials** to make many different things. Some solids, such as stone, are hard and strong and are good for building. Other solids, such as feathers, are soft and are perfect for filling pillows and cushions. Some solids are stretchy, like elastic, but others, like wood, do not stretch at all. Some, like metal, can be sharpened. Some, like plastics, can be moulded into different shapes and dyed bright colours. All these materials are very different, but they are all solids.

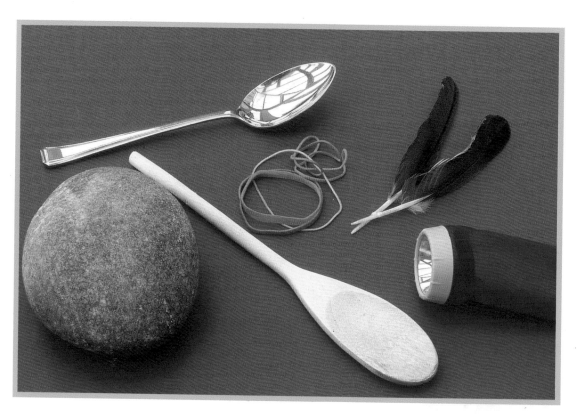

Life-giving water

The most important liquid is water. We need to drink a lot of water to keep our bodies healthy. We also use water for cooking, and for many other things too – for washing ourselves and the things we use, swimming and playing in swimming pools, sailing and surfing on lakes and the sea. Water spraying into the air from fountains makes our parks and gardens look attractive. Farmers and gardeners spray water onto crops and other plants to help them to grow.

Using other liquids

Many other things around us are liquids too. Tomato ketchup, hot custard and orange juice are tasty liquids to eat and drink, and we can use cooking oil for frying foods like chips. Our pens would not write without ink and motor car engines need petrol. We use oil to keep our **machines** working smoothly and washing-up liquid to clean our dirty dishes. Lots of things that we use to keep ourselves clean are liquids, such as shampoo and shower-gel.

Using gases

Most gases are invisible but that does not mean they are not important. When we breathe in, we take in a gas called oxygen from the air to stay alive. We get rid of waste carbon dioxide when we breathe out. We put carbon dioxide into some drinks like lemonade to make them fizzy. We pump air into the tyres of cars and bicycles to cushion us from bumpy rides. Helium is a gas that is lighter than air so a balloon filled with helium will float away unless you hold it down. Many houses have gas fires and gas cookers that burn natural gas, giving out heat that can be used for heating or cooking. Camp stoves and gas barbecues use other gases, such as propane, as fuel.

Air

The atmosphere which surrounds the Earth is a layer of air about 500 km thick. Without the atmosphere, nothing could live on Earth. The air is made up of a mixture of different gases. Nitrogen makes up just under four-fifths of the air, one-fifth is oxygen and then there are tiny amounts of other gases such as carbon dioxide and argon.

What are solids, liquids and gases made from?

Everything around us is made of very tiny pieces. The tiniest pieces of anything that can exist are called **atoms**. These are joined together to make bigger pieces called **molecules**. It is hard to imagine, but molecules are so tiny that there are millions and millions in a single grain of sand. Each **material** is made up from its own special molecules. The molecules in solids, liquids and gases are arranged in different ways.

Patterns of molecules

In a solid, the molecules are all lined up in a tight, regular pattern. They are very close together and each one is held in its place by the other molecules around it. They cannot move around at all.

The molecules are freer in a liquid than in a solid. They are spaced out and arranged in a loose pattern. They are not held together tightly, so they can move about and change places with other molecules close to them.

Molecules of gases are not held together at all. They move about **randomly** all the time and are not arranged in a pattern.

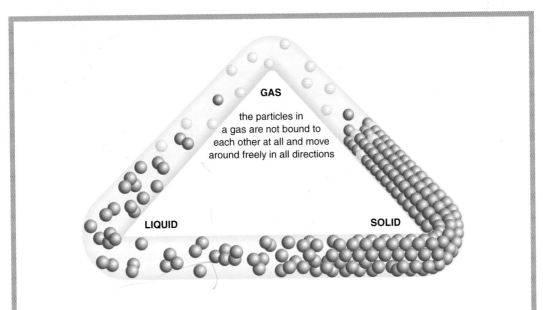

GAS

the particles in a gas are not bound to each other at all and move around freely in all directions

LIQUID

SOLID

EXPERIMENT: Why will water change colour when liquid coloured dye is added?

HYPOTHESIS:
The molecules of the dye are able to move through the water and spread out. This movement results in colour being seen throughout the water.

EQUIPMENT:
Coloured food dye (washable if possible), cold water, a clear plastic container and a pipette or eye dropper.

EXPERIMENT STEPS:
1　Half fill your container with cold water.
2　Stand it carefully on a table and wait until the water looks absolutely still.
3　Suck up a few drops of dye with your pipette or eye dropper.
4　Put one or two drops carefully onto the water.
5　Watch what happens.
6　Write down what you saw.

CONCLUSION:
There are spaces between molecules in a liquid and they are able to move around. Because two liquids were mixed, their molecules could mix together freely and so the colour spreads throughout the water.

How do solids, liquids and gases move and change?

Solids, liquids and gases all move and change in different ways. There are three questions we can ask about something to find out whether it is a solid, a liquid or a gas.

1. Does it change its shape?

Solids only change their shape if a **force** is applied to them. A lump of modelling clay keeps its shape until you pull and push, squeeze and stretch it into a new shape. But liquids and gases do not keep their shape. If you pour runny orange juice out of a carton into a glass, it spreads out to take the shape of the glass exactly. When you blow up a balloon, the air you breathe out spreads out to completely fill the shape of the balloon.

2. Does it flow?

Solids cannot flow because their **molecules** are held together too tightly. But liquids and gases can flow easily. You can pour a liquid from one container into another container – for example, when you turn on a tap, water flows out of the pipe and into your glass. Liquids spread out on their own, too – if you spill some paint, it does not just stay in a lump but flows and spreads out to cover a bigger space. Gases also flow freely, as you can see when you untie the knot on a balloon and the air inside flows freely out.

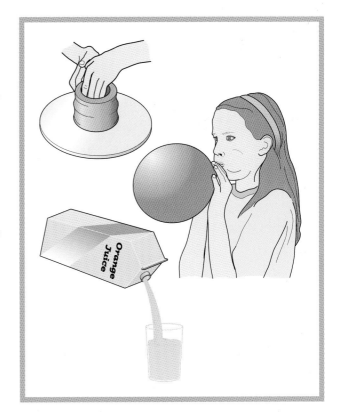

3. Does it always take up the same amount of space?

The amount of space something takes up is called its **volume**. A solid brick does not change its shape so it will always have the same volume.

If you pour a litre of milk out of a carton into a measuring jug, it will be a different shape but there will still be exactly one litre of milk. So liquids change their shape but always have the same volume.

When air freshener is sprayed out of a can at one side of a room, it slowly spreads across the room until eventually people right at the other side will be able to smell it. This is because gases do not always have the same volume. They spread out to fill all the space they possibly can.

By asking these three questions, you can decide whether something is a solid, a liquid or a gas.

This table shows the answers:

question	solids	liquids	gases
Does it change its shape?	no	yes	yes
Does it flow?	no	yes	yes
Does it always have the same volume?	yes	yes	no

DEMONSTRATION: The temperature of a liquid can affect how fast it will flow.

EQUIPMENT:
You will need: a 30 cm ruler, something to lean the ruler on (such as a large book in a plastic bag, or a pencil case), honey, an eyedropper, a stopwatch or wristwatch with a second hand, a small drinking glass, a tablespoon and a small bowl of hot water.

DEMONSTRATION STEPS:
1 With the ruler flat on the table, put some honey on it to fill the space between 1 and 2.
2 Carefully lean the ruler against the book with the 0 at the top and start the clock.
3 Write down how far the honey travelled in 10 seconds.
4 Wash your ruler.
5 Put two tablespoons of honey in the drinking glass. Stand the glass in the bowl of hot water. You may have to steady it to keep it from tipping. Let the honey warm up for about 3 or 4 minutes.
6 Repeat steps 1, 2 and 3 with the warmed up honey.

7 Write down what you saw.

EXPLANATION:
Warming up a liquid will make it flow faster because the molecules are moving around faster and through greater distances within the liquid.

Can solids become liquids?

We can keep things cold in a freezer. When you take something out of the freezer, it is hard and solid. When we take ice-cubes out of the freezer into a warmer place, the solid ice slowly turns into liquid. When this happens, we say the ice **melts**. Ice and liquid water are made up of exactly the same **molecules** – the only difference is that the molecules are arranged in a different way. This is a **physical change** and is called a **change of state**.

Melting ice lollies

If you don't eat your ice lolly quickly enough on a hot day, it will melt and drip all over the place! The heat from the air around you melts the frozen fruit juice, changing it from a solid into a liquid.

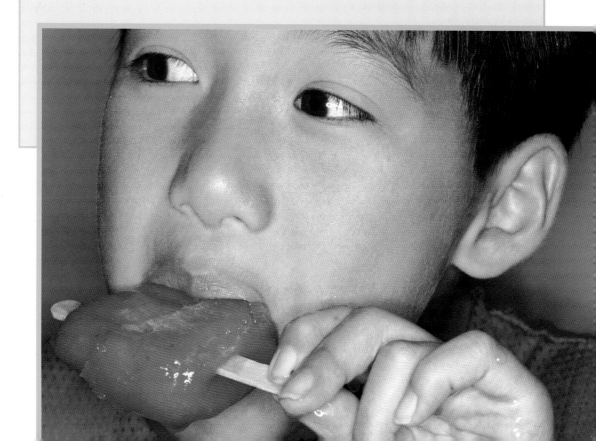

Back and forth

Changing state from a solid to a liquid is a **reversible** change. This means that it can go backwards or forwards – we can change a solid to a liquid and then change the liquid back into a solid again!

Getting colder . . .

When we cool a liquid down, it gets colder and colder until at last it changes into a solid. This change is called **freezing**. Water freezes at 0 °C and so this is its freezing point. If you put liquid water into an ice-cube tray and put it into the freezer, it will turn into solid ice.

Other liquids change into solids as they cool down too. Different liquids become solids at different temperatures. Liquid wax from a candle may drip down but as it cools it will turn back into solid wax. Liquid rock pours out of a volcano but changes into solid rock as it cools.

Freezing cold!

You can see things freezing all around you in the winter. Puddles freeze and water drips to form icicles. When the air is cold, rain freezes and falls as snow or hail.

Can liquids become gases?

We can heat liquids up too. They get hotter and hotter until at last they cannot stay as a liquid any more and they change into a gas. The liquid and the gas are made up of exactly the same **molecules** – the only difference is that the molecules are arranged in a different way. This is another **change of state**. The gas molecules go into the air around them. When this happens, we say the liquid **evaporates**. The more quickly we heat a liquid, the more quickly it evaporates.

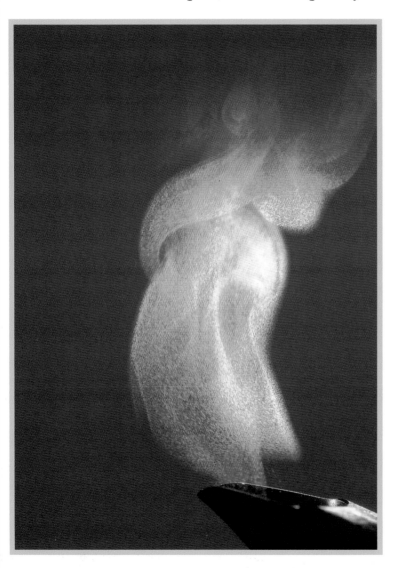

Boiling water

When you boil water in a kettle, it gets hotter and hotter. When the temperature of the water reaches 100 °C, the water boils. This is the boiling point of water. The water cannot stay as a liquid when it is this hot and it turns into the gas that we call steam or water **vapour**. Different liquids have different boiling points at which they turn into gas.

Changing a liquid into a gas is a **reversible** change – if we cool a gas down, it will turn back into a liquid.

If you breathe out hard on a cold day, you can see a stream of white blowing into the air. The warm air from inside your body cools quickly when it mixes with the cold air outside. Water vapour in your breath turns back into liquid water – and you see the tiny droplets of liquid water. Changing back from a gas into a liquid is called **condensing**.

All steamed up!

When a gas cools down, it turns back into a liquid. Water evaporates from the hot bath and becomes water vapour. When the water vapour hits a cold surface like the glass window or mirror, it cools down very quickly. It turns back into liquid water that you see as a misty layer.

Some **materials** can only change their state if they are very hot or very cold.

Most metals need to be heated to a very high temperature before they will **melt** and turn into liquids. Gold has to be heated to more than 1000 °C for it to melt, and iron does not melt until it is hotter than 1500 °C. That is really hot – nearly eight times hotter than your oven needs to be to cook a pizza!

Most gases need to be extremely cold before they will change into liquids. Both oxygen and nitrogen change from gas to liquid at nearly -200 °C – that is about ten times colder than an ordinary freezer!

An unusual gas

Carbon dioxide is an unusual gas because it changes straight from a solid to a gas without being a liquid in between. Chunks of solid carbon dioxide are sometimes used in theatres – as the solid warms up, white clouds of gas slowly waft across the stage creating eerie, misty effects.

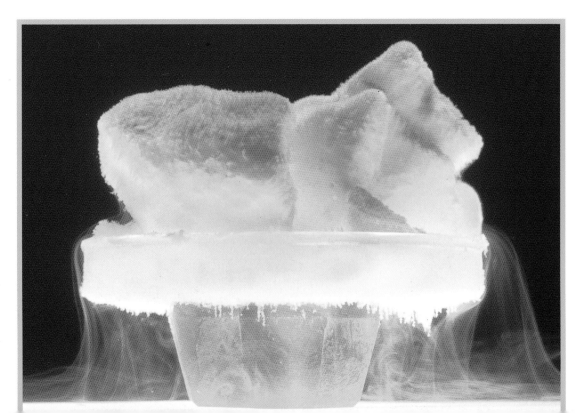

EXPERIMENT: How can a solid be changed to a liquid?

HYPOTHESIS:
Warming a substance will change its **state of matter**.

EQUIPMENT:
A few ice-cubes, three plastic beakers, a thermometer and a scale.

EXPERIMENT STEPS:
1 Put the ice-cubes in the three beakers and push the thermometer down into one beaker. Measure and write down the temperature.
2 Weigh one beaker with the ice-cubes. Write down the weight.
3 Put the beakers of ice-cubes in a warm place, perhaps in the sun on a window-sill.
4 Leave one beaker for 10 minutes, another beaker for 20 minutes and the third for 30 minutes. Measure the temperature of the melted ice-cubes in each beaker. Weigh each beaker.
5 Write down the temperatures and weights.

CONCLUSION:
As the temperature increased the ice changed from solid to liquid. The weight of the ice and the water after the ice melted were the same. No matter was lost or gained when the ice changed from solid to liquid.

ADDITIONAL EXPERIMENTS:
You could try starting with more or less ice-cubes, or using a different type of container – do they make any difference?

What is the Water Cycle?

Water is very important to every living thing – without water, nothing could live. Water covers 71 per cent of our planet. Some, such as water in the oceans and seas, is salty. Some, such as water in lakes and rivers, is not salty. All around us, every minute of every day, water is moving and changing from solid to liquid to gas and back again. These changes that go round and round and never stop are called the 'Water Cycle'.

Let's start with the sea ...

When the Sun shines on the sea water, it warms it up. Some water gets so warm that it **evaporates**. It turns from liquid water into water **vapour**. This warm water vapour rises higher and higher.

The higher the water vapour rises, the colder the air around it gets. This cools the water vapour. At last, the water vapour gets so cold that it turns back into liquid water. These droplets of liquid water form clouds.

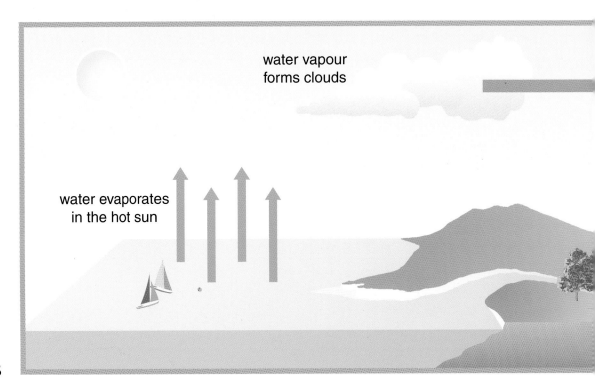

water vapour
forms clouds

water evaporates
in the hot sun

Clouds get blown across the sky by the wind. Water droplets in the clouds group together to make bigger droplets. When they get too big, they fall down to Earth as rain. As the clouds rise higher in the sky, they get colder and colder. If the clouds get really cold, the water droplets may turn into ice **crystals**. These fall to Earth as snowflakes or hailstones. Water falling to Earth as rain, snow or hail is called **precipitation**. Most of the rain seeps through the land into streams or rivers, which flow to the sea. Then the cycle begins again.

Rain, streams and rivers

Some rain soaks into the rocks and reappears as a spring further on. Some rain trickles over the surface of the ground, making tiny streams. These join together to make rivers. All the rivers flow back to the sea – and the whole cycle begins again.

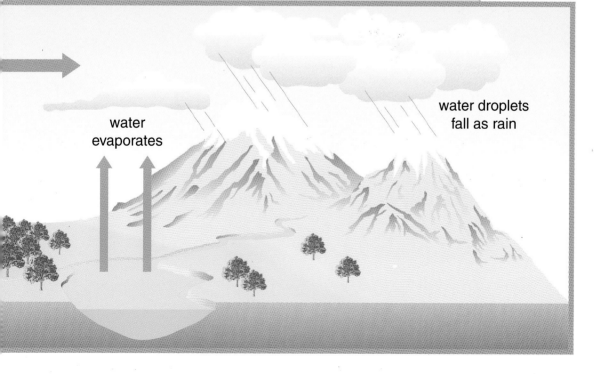

water evaporates

water droplets fall as rain

EXPERIMENT: How are clouds formed?

HYPOTHESIS:
Clouds are formed when water vapour cools.

EQUIPMENT:
A tall glass jar with a metal lid (such as a jamjar or pickle jar), hot (not boiling) water, a few ice-cubes, cling film.

EXPERIMENT STEPS:
1 Wrap some ice-cubes in cling film.
2 Half-fill your jar with hot water. (It is a good idea to get an adult to help you.)
3 Put the lid on the jar.
4 Put your parcel of ice cubes on top of the lid.
5 Watch what happens inside the jar just under the lid.

7 Write down what you saw.

CONCLUSION:
When water vapour cools down, it **condenses** into water droplets. This is how clouds are formed. The ice-cubes cool the water vapour in the jar in exactly the same way that the cold air in the atmosphere cools the warm water vapour that rises from the sea.

Can all changes go backwards and forwards?

Physical changes of state are **reversible**. This means they can go backwards and forwards, for example we can change water into ice and ice back into water. Not all changes can do this. Some can only go one way and can never go backwards. These **irreversible** changes are **chemical changes**.

Burning is a chemical change that can only go one way. When we burn wood, the bright flames provide light and warmth. Smoke spirals up into the air. When the fire goes out, we are left with just a pile of ashes. This is all that is left of the wood. It has been changed for ever and we cannot get back the wood that we started with.

Clay and pottery

Potters use clay to make their pots and jugs. While the clay is soft and wet, they can make it into all sorts of shapes. Then they put it into a very hot oven called a kiln. When the clay comes out of the kiln, it is dry and hard. The potter cannot get the soft, wet clay back. It has changed for ever.

Irreversible changes happen when we cook things. If you fry an egg, you can never change it back into a raw egg, can you? And once bread has been toasted, it can never be changed back into ordinary bread again.

Plaster models

You can make models using a fine white powder called **plaster of Paris**. When this is mixed with water, it makes a runny white liquid. If you pour it into a **mould** and leave it for a while, it slowly becomes hard and solid. The water **molecules** become locked to the plaster molecules and cannot be separated. When you take it out of the mould, it keeps the shape of the mould it was in. You can paint and decorate your model – but you cannot get the white powder back again. This is an irreversible, chemical change.

Burning, cooking, making pottery and plaster models are just some of the ways we use chemical changes. Many other things that we do involve chemical changes too.

A complete change

Some chemical changes make new **materials**. Heating sand and limestone makes glass. When they get very hot, a chemical change happens and they turn into glass. Some special types of glue come in two separate tubes. When you mix the substances from the two tubes together, there is a chemical change. The new material that is made makes a very, very strong join.

Dyes are special chemicals that we use to change the colour of things. When you mix the fabric with the dye, a chemical change binds them together so the colour of the fabric changes. **Bleaches** do the opposite. They change the dyes so that the colours fade or go completely, leaving a faded or white fabric.

Photographs

When you take a photograph using an ordinary camera, a chemical change happens as light hits the photographic film. More chemical changes are needed to finally develop and print your pictures from the film.

DEMONSTRATION: Baking soda is a solid in the form of a powder. Lemon juice is a liquid. If you combine them, a chemical change will take place.

EQUIPMENT:
You will need: a clear plastic tube or bottle with a small neck, lemon juice, sodium bicarbonate (baking soda) and a balloon.

DEMONSTRATION STEPS:
(Hint: this can get messy so it's a good idea to do it over a sink or large bowl.)

1 Pour some lemon juice into your bottle.
2 Add a teaspoon of sodium bicarbonate.
3 Quickly fit the balloon over the neck of the bottle.
4 Watch what happens.
5 The fizziness shows that a chemical reaction is taking place.

6 Write down what you saw.

EXPLANATION:
When you add sodium bicarbonate to lemon juice, you can see that a chemical change takes place because the liquid and powder make a gas. The gas rises up out of the bottle and fills the balloon.

What is a solution?

If you stir a teaspoon of sugar into a cup of water, the sugar will slowly disappear. The water stays clear and the sugar vanishes. If you taste the water, though, it will be sweet – so the sugar must still be there, even if you cannot see it. When you add sugar to water, you create a **mixture.** When sugar mixes with water this way, we say the solid has **dissolved.** The sugary water is called a sugar **solution**.

In some mixtures, such as rice and sand, you can always see both substances clearly. So, all solutions are mixtures, but not all mixtures are solutions.

Mixing other solids with water

Sugar is not the only solid that dissolves in water. Usually, we add sugar to hot drinks such as tea or coffee. The hotter the liquid, the faster the **molecules** move around. This makes the spaces between them bigger so the sugar molecules can find a space more quickly. It takes much longer to dissolve sugar in cold water than in hot water.

The form that the sugar is in affects how quickly it dissolves. Sugar grains dissolve more quickly than lumps or cubes. This is because the separate grains can spread out through the water more quickly than bigger lumps. Other solids can dissolve too. For example, the sea is a solution made of water with salt dissolved in it. Some solids will not dissolve in water but will dissolve in a different liquid such as alcohol or oil.

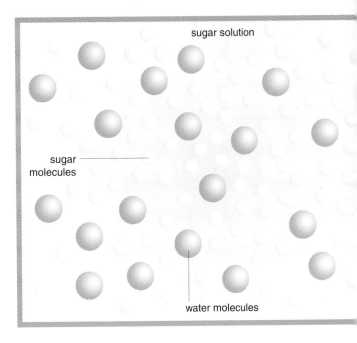

sugar solution

sugar molecules

water molecules

Solution or suspension

Sometimes a solid does not dissolve in the liquid, but it does not settle to the bottom, either. It also does not float on top of the liquid. The molecules of the solid float throughout the liquid and give it a cloudy **appearance**. We call this a **suspension**. If a suspension is left undisturbed for a while, the solid will eventually sink to the bottom.

Stirring things up ...

Stirring liquids speeds up dissolving too. It spreads the molecules of the solid throughout the liquid so they can find the spaces more quickly.

DEMONSTRATION: You can make your own solutions, mixtures and suspensions.

EQUIPMENT:

You will need: five disposable plastic containers, five disposable plastic spoons, water, one teaspoon of each of: sugar, sand, salt, flour, **plaster of Paris**.

DEMONSTRATION STEPS:

1 Half-fill each container with water.
2 Put one teaspoon of sugar into the first container and stir. Repeat, putting sand into the second container, salt into the third, flour into the fourth and plaster of Paris into the fifth.
3 Leave them to stand for about 30 minutes.
4 Write down what you see happening in each container.

EXPLANATION:

Some solids dissolve in water, but others do not. Sand molecules are much larger and heavier than those of water, so the sand sinks to the bottom. Sugar water and salt water are solutions; sand and water form a mixture; flour and plaster of Paris each form suspensions when mixed with water.

People who found the answers

John Dalton (1766-1844)

John Dalton was an English scientist. One of his most important ideas was his Atomic Theory, which said that everything is made up of tiny pieces called **atoms**. He tried to use this idea to explain how solids and liquids move and change, and how **chemical changes** happen.

Joseph Priestley (1733-1804)

Joseph Priestley was an English church minister who also did a lot of experiments. He discovered nitrogen and oxygen (although a Swedish scientist called Scheele said he had actually discovered oxygen first). Joseph also invented the first fizzy soft drink!

Antoine Lavoisier (1743-1794)

Antoine Lavoisier lived and worked in France. He was a scientist and a politician. One of his most important discoveries was how oxygen is important in burning and breathing. He also developed one of the first systems for naming chemicals.

Amazing facts

- You might find it hard to believe, but glass is really a liquid! You cannot see it flowing, because it is very, very thick and flows extremely slowly. Over hundreds of years, it will slowly flow downwards – so very old glass windows are thicker at the bottom than at the top!

- Water does not always boil at exactly 100 °C! At sea level, the boiling point of water is 100 °C, but as you climb higher, the boiling point gets lower. At the top of Mount Everest, which is nearly 9 km (5.5 miles) above sea level, the boiling point is only 71 °C. This is because the higher you go, the lower the pressure of the air – so the water molecules can escape more easily into the air.

- Not all planets are made of rock! Saturn is nearly all gas, and is so light that it would float on water.

- The first person to understand what volume meant was Archimedes, a scientist in ancient Greece. When he got into his bath, he realized that his body made the level of the water rise. The amount of water pushed up was exactly the same as the amount of space his body took up – his volume.

- The largest hailstone ever recorded was found in the US state of Kansas. It was an amazing 19 cm across and weighed 758 g!

- Snowflakes are tiny crystals of ice. Each one has six arms – and no two snowflakes are ever identical!

▷• Glossary

appearance what something or someone looks like

atom one of the tiny particles of which matter is made

bleach chemical used to remove unwanted colour or stains

change of state change from one state of matter to another

chemical change change in which something new is made

condense cool a gas so that it turns into a liquid

crystal hard mineral that looks like glass

dissolve what happens when a solid becomes part of a solution

evaporate what a liquid does to turn into a vapour

force something that changes or moves an object

freeze cool a liquid so that it turns into a solid

irreversible change that can only go one way

machine anything made to help human beings do some task, such as a car, a computer or an electric drill

material any substance you can use to make something else

melt heat a solid so that it turns into a liquid

mixture result of mixing two or more materials together

molecule two or more atoms joined together

mould container that holds a liquid to be set into a particular shape

physical change change from one state of matter to another

plaster of Paris fine white powder that can be mixed with water to make models

precipitation when water falls to Earth as rain, snow or hail

randomly something that happens in a disorganized, uncontrolled way

reversible change that can go backwards or forwards

solution liquid that has a solid dissolved in it

state of matter whether a material is a solid, a liquid or a gas

suspension liquid that has particles of a solid hanging in it

vapour material in its gas state, which some liquids change to as they evaporate

volume amount of space that something takes up

Index

More books to read

Materials All Around Us: Solids, Liquids and Gases, Robert Snedden (Heinemann Library, 2001)
Chemicals in Action: Solids, Liquids and Gases, Chris Oxlade (Heinemann Library, 2002)
Material World: Solids, Liquids & Gases, Robert Snedden (Heinemann Library, 2002)
ChemLab: Gases, Liquids and Solids, Keith Walshaw (Atlantic Europe Publishing Co Ltd, 1998)